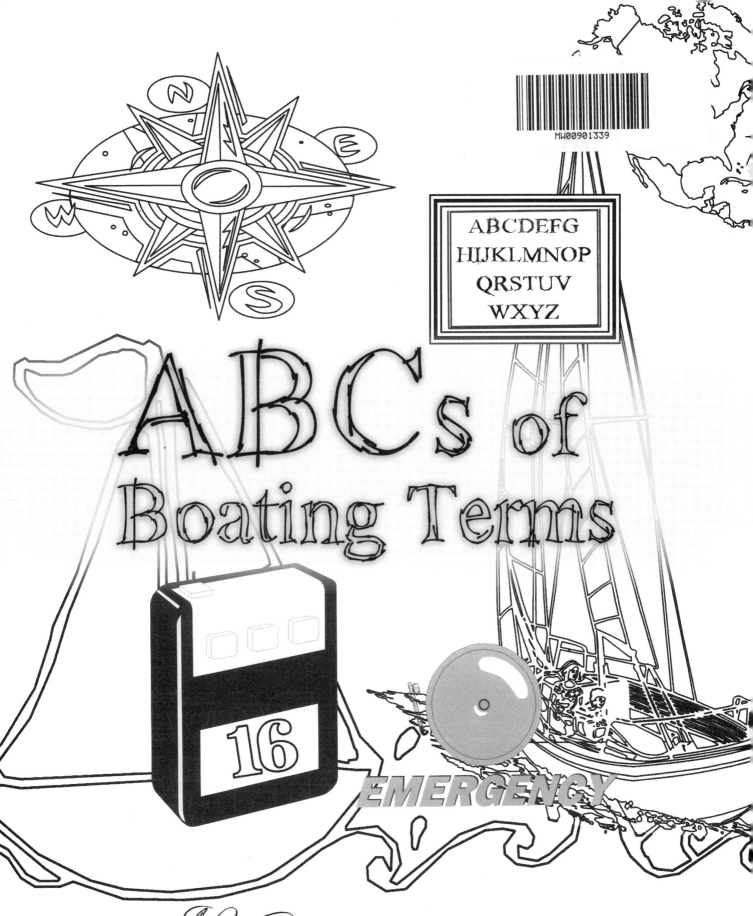

ABCDEFG
HIJKLMNOP
QRSTUV
WXYZ

ABCs of
Boating Terms

16

EMERGENCY

Schiffer
Publishing Ltd

4880 Lower Valley Road, Atglen, Pennsylvania 19310

Created and Written
by Dee Cache

Introduction

For all children and those who want to be...

I created this coloring book to help you learn boating terms and safety tips in a fun, easy-to-understand way. Now everyone can enjoy art and nautical knowledge at the same time.

You can use colored pencils, crayons, marking pens, watercolor, or acrylic paints and enjoy your artistic works for many years to come.

Enjoy,

Dee

Other Schiffer Books By The Author:
Captain Tugalong, 978-0-8703-3515-0, $12.95

Other Schiffer Books on Related Subjects:
U.S. Life Saving Coloring Book, 978-0-7643-3483-2, $6.99
Windmills Activity Book, 978-0-7643-3455-9, $6.99

Designed by Mark David Bowyer
Type set in !Sketchy Times / Zurich BT

ISBN: 978-0-7643-3982-0
Printed in the United States of America

Schiffer Books are available at special discounts for bulk purchases for sales promotions or premiums. Special editions, including personalized covers, corporate imprints, and excerpts can be created in large quantities for special needs. For more information contact the publisher:

Published by Schiffer Publishing Ltd.
4880 Lower Valley Road
Atglen, PA 19310
Phone: (610) 593-1777; Fax: (610) 593-2002
E-mail: Info@schifferbooks.com

For the largest selection of fine reference books on this and related subjects, please visit our website at
www.schifferbooks.com
We are always looking for people to write books on new and related subjects. If you have an idea for a book, please contact us at
proposals@schifferbooks.com

This book may be purchased from the publisher.
Include $5.00 for shipping.
Please try your bookstore first.
You may write for a free catalog.

In Europe, Schiffer books are distributed by
Bushwood Books
6 Marksbury Ave.
Kew Gardens
Surrey TW9 4JF England
Phone: 44 (0) 20 8392 8585; Fax: 44 (0) 20 8392 9876
E-mail: info@bushwoodbooks.co.uk
Website: www.bushwoodbooks.co.uk

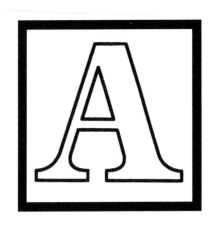

AFT

THE REAR PART OF A BOAT

BOW

(Rhymes with HOW)

THE FRONT PART OF THE BOAT

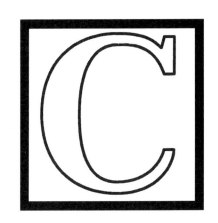

COMPASS

SHOWS US WHICH WAY TO GO

DECK D

THE FLOOR
OF A BOAT

ENGINE

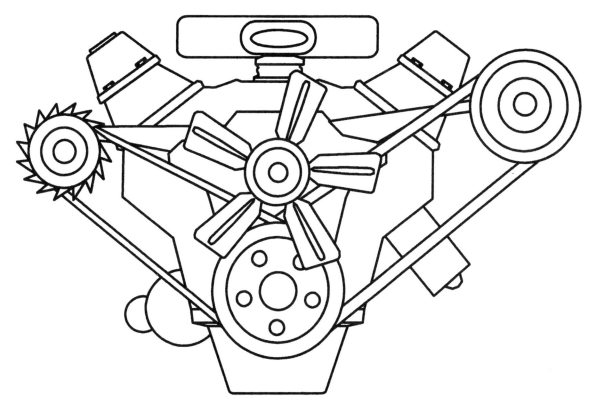

A MACHINE THAT MAKES ENERGY TO MOVE THE BOAT

FORE

THE FRONT PART OF THE BOAT

NAUTICAL FLAGS CAN SPELL WORDS. THIS IS THE FLAG FOR THE LETTER "F"

FLAGS

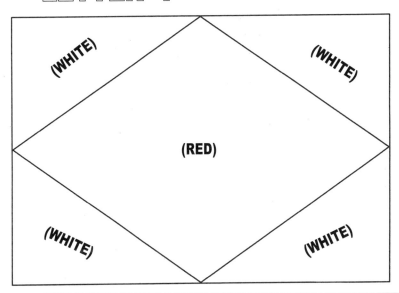

(WHITE)   (WHITE)

(RED)

(WHITE)   (WHITE)

NAUTICAL FLAGS FOR HELP

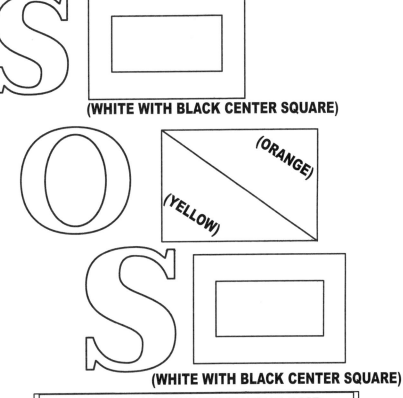

S (WHITE WITH BLACK CENTER SQUARE)

O (ORANGE) (YELLOW)

S (WHITE WITH BLACK CENTER SQUARE)

IF YOU ARE IN TROUBLE AND NEED HELP USE THE S-O-S FLAGS

GALLEY

THE KITCHEN ON A BOAT

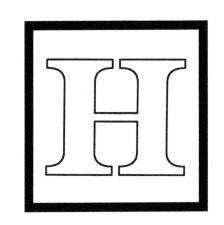

ON A BOAT, THE BATHROOM IS CALLED THE HEAD

NAUTICAL FLAGS CAN SPELL OUT MESSAGES. THIS IS THE FLAG FOR THE LETTER "I"

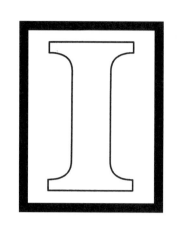

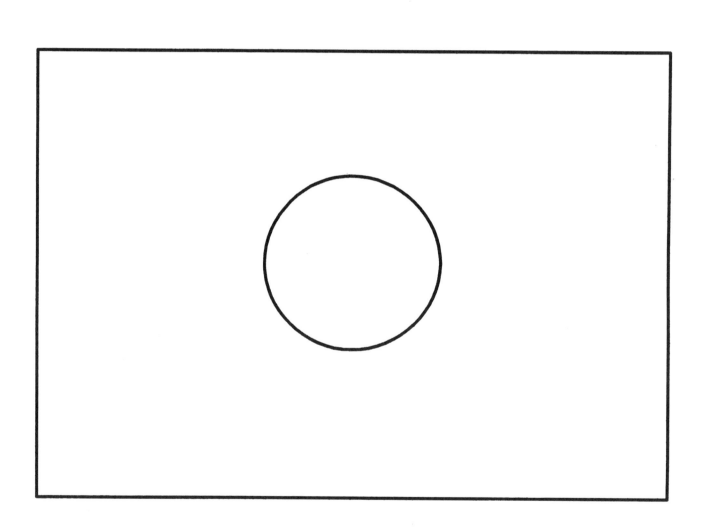

COLOR THIS FLAG YELLOW WITH A BLACK DOT

NAUTICAL FLAGS SPELL WORDS. THIS IS THE NAUTICAL FLAG FOR THE LETTER "J"

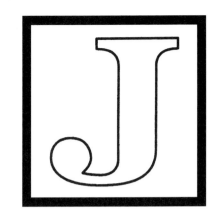

(BLACK)

(WHITE)

(BLACK)

KAYAK

A CANOE MADE OF SKINS STRETCHED OVER WOOD

LINE

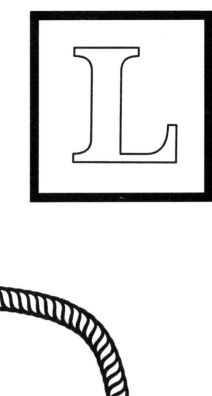

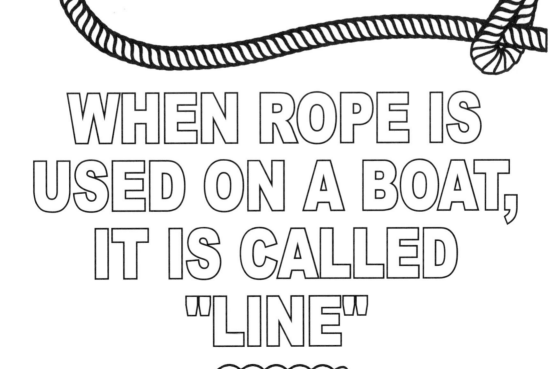

WHEN ROPE IS USED ON A BOAT, IT IS CALLED "LINE"

MAYDAY
MEANS
HELP ME !

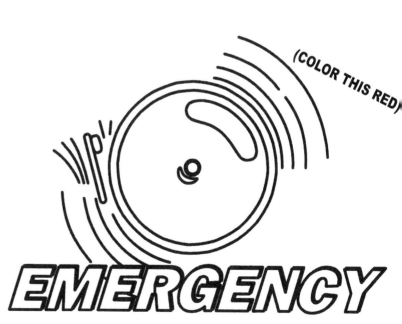

(COLOR THIS RED)

EMERGENCY

Channel 16 is the emergency radio channel all over the world

NAVIGATE

PLANNING THE COURSE
WHERE YOU WANT
YOUR BOAT TO GO

OAR

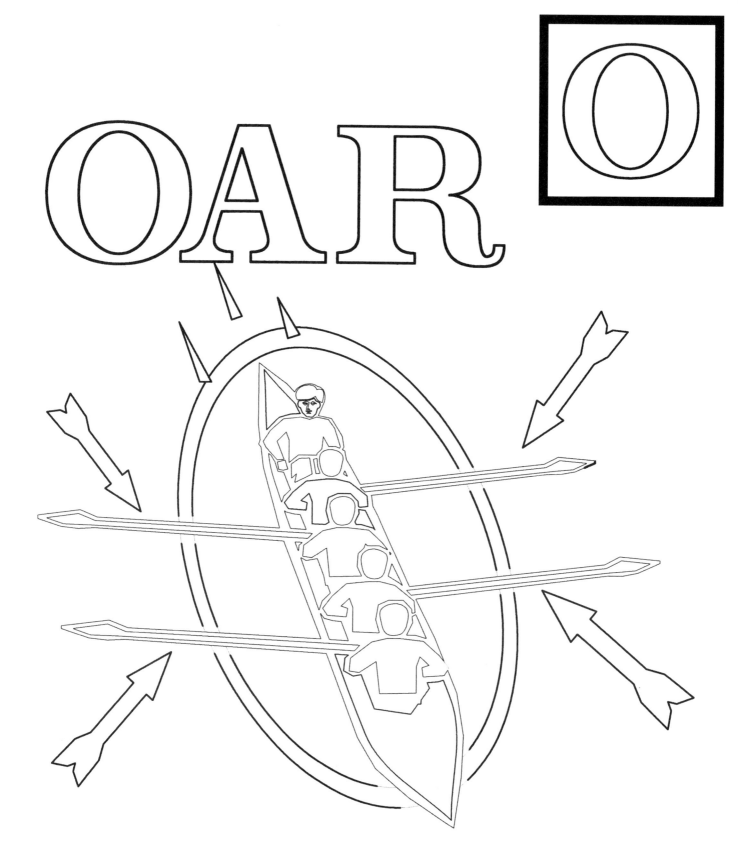

OARS HELP THE BOAT MOVE IN THE WATER

PORT SIDE

An easy way to remember this word: **PORT** and **LEFT** both have 4 letters

THE LEFT SIDE OF A BOAT

THE PERSON WHO WEARS THIS HAT IS CALLED THE CAPTAIN

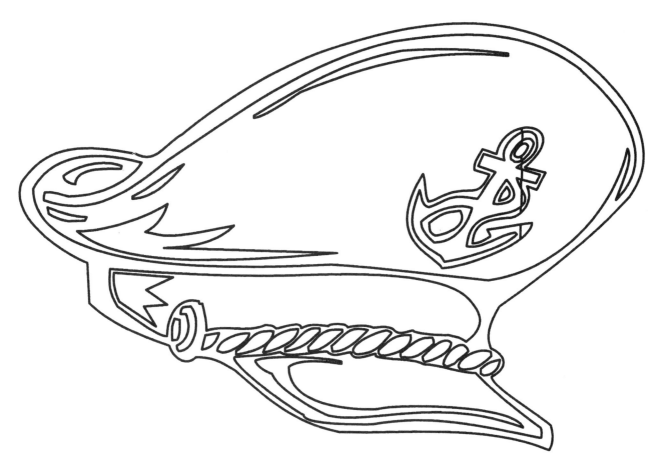

ON A BOAT THE CAPTAIN IS ALWAYS IN CHARGE

QUARTER DECK

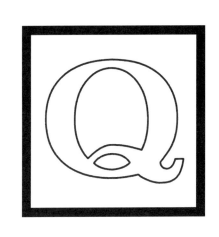

THE AFTER PART OF THE UPPER DECK ON A NAVAL VESSEL USUALLY RESERVED FOR OFFICERS

RAILING

**TO HELP KEEP OUR BALANCE
AND PROTECT US FROM
FALLING INTO THE WATER**

THESE ARE SAILBOATS

BOATS ARE NOT PLACES TO LEAVE YOUR TRASH

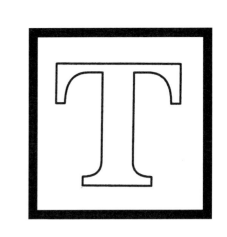

PUT TRASH IN PLASTIC BAGS AND THROW AWAY IN RECEPTACLES WHEN YOU RETURN TO LAND

SPELLING OUT WORDS WITH FLAGS HELP US TALK TO OTHER BOATS.

RED	WHITE
WHITE	RED

THIS IS THE NAUTICAL FLAG FOR THE LETTER "U"

WEATHER VANE

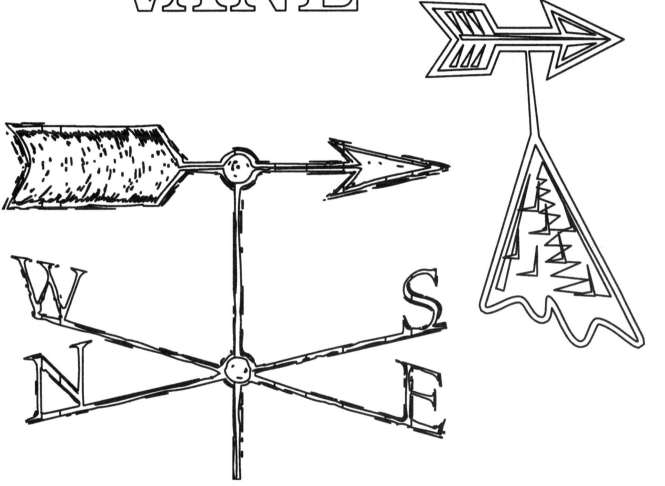

A WEATHER VANE
WILL TELL YOU IN
WHICH DIRECTION
THE WIND IS BLOWING

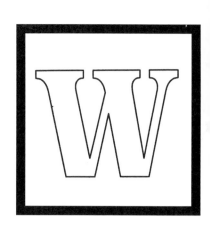

WAKE

WAVES THAT ARE MADE BY A MOVING BOAT

IT IS VERY DANGEROUS TO BE BAREFOOT ON A BOAT

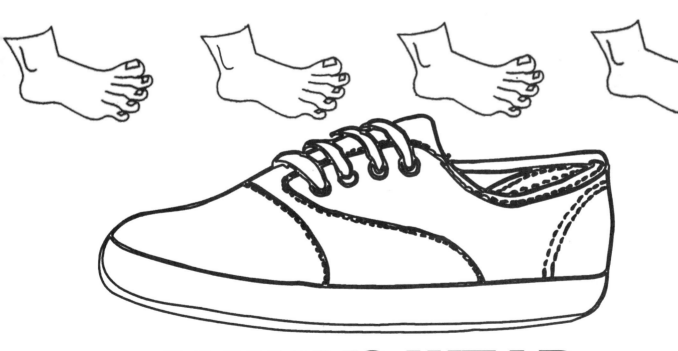

ALWAYS WEAR SHOES ON A BOAT

XEBEK X

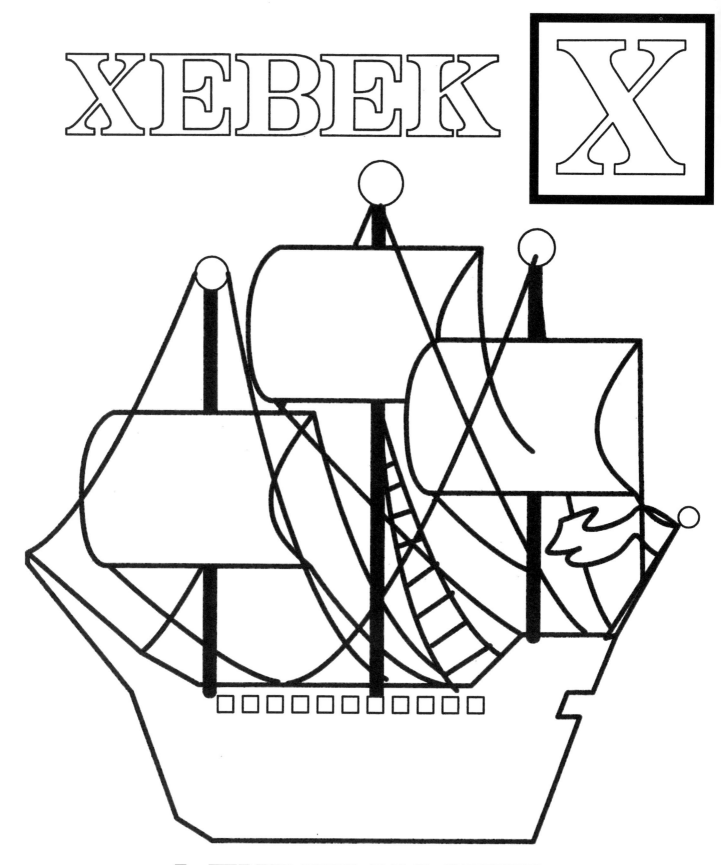

A THREE MASTED
MEDITERRANEAN
SAILING VESSEL

THIS IS A YACHT

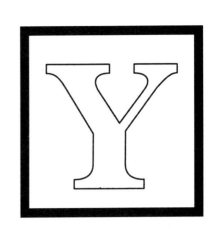

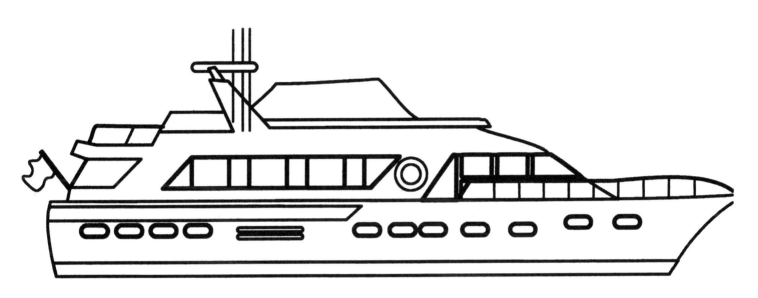

THIS IS A YACHTING HAT

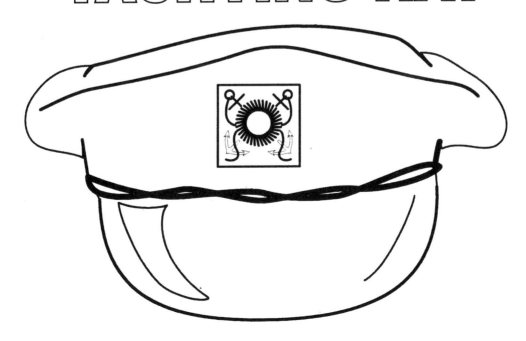

NAUTICAL FLAGS CAN SPELL OUT MESSAGES. THIS IS THE FLAG FOR THE LETTER "Z"

(YELLOW)

(BROWN)

(BROWN)

(ORANGE)